GW01191465

Chester String Series

Graded Violin Pieces
Volume 1 (1st. Position)

Arranged and Edited by

Peggy Radmall

1.	Tower Hill	Giles Farnaby
2.	His rest	Giles Farnaby
3.	Gavotte	G. F. Handel
4.	Chanson Favorite d'Henri IV	Traditional
5.	Minuet and Trio	W. A. Mozart
6.	The St. Catherine	John Barrett
7.	Saraband	John Barrett
8.	Rigaudons	Henri Desmarets
9.	Two German Dances	W. A. Mozart
10.	The Lark	M. Glinka

Extra Violin parts available

Chester Music
(A Music Sales Limited Company)
8/9 Frith Street, London, W1V 5TZ

TOWER HILL

VIOLIN

GILES FARNABY
(*c.* 1560–*c.* 1600)

HIS REST

GILES FARNABY

VIOLIN

GAVOTTE

G. F. HANDEL
(1685-1759)

CHANSON FAVORITE D'HENRI IV

VIOLIN

Traditional

Allegro cantabile

MINUET AND TRIO

VIOLIN

W. A. MOZART
(1756-91)

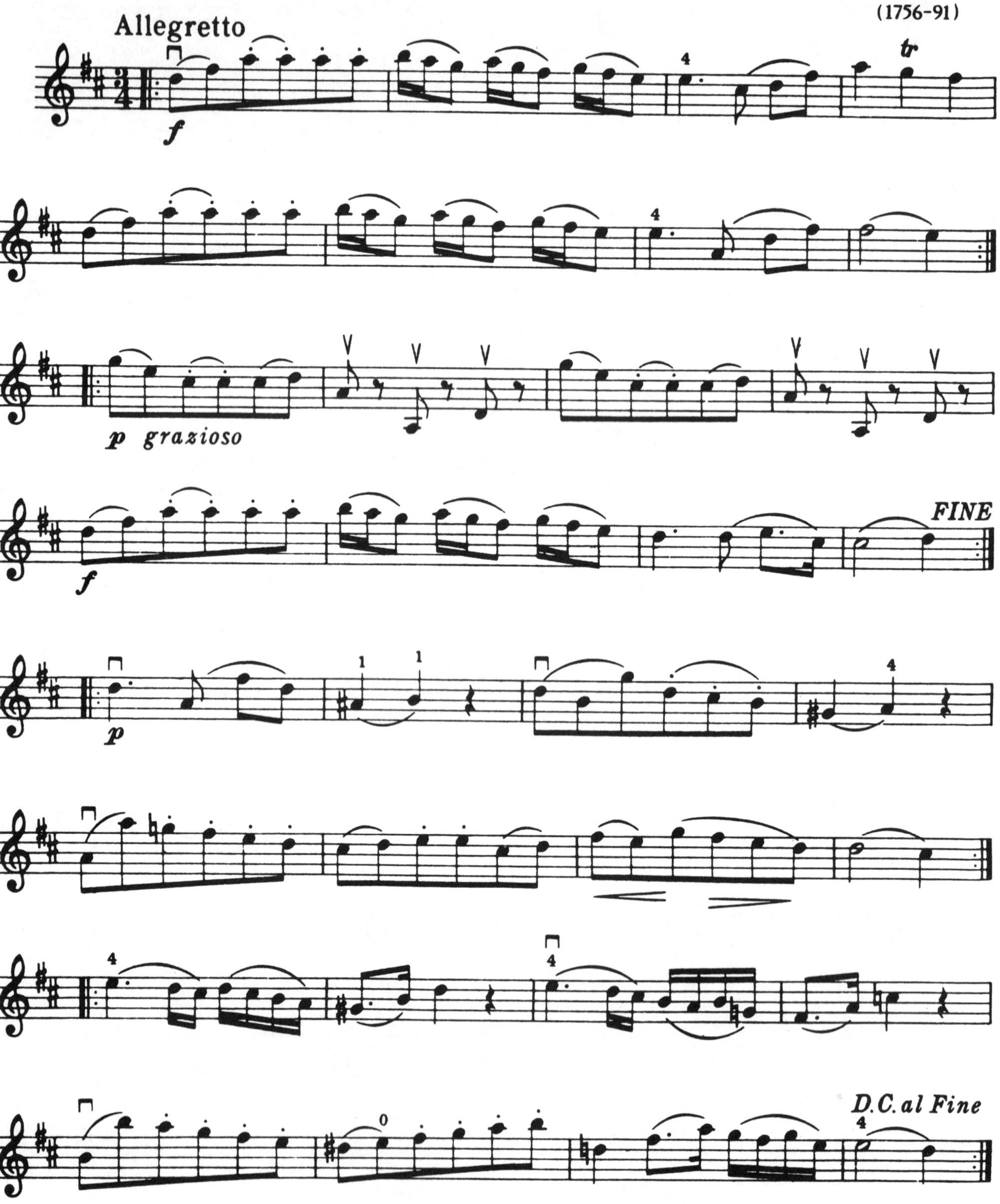

THE St CATHERINE

VIOLIN

JOHN BARRETT
(*c.* 1674–*c.* 1735)

Allegretto vivace

SARABAND

JOHN BARRETT
(*c.* 1674–*c.* 1735)

Andante espressivo

RIGAUDONS

VIOLIN

HENRI DESMARETS
(*c.* 1662-1741)

TWO GERMAN DANCES

VIOLIN

1

MOZART
(1756-91)

The sign ⌿ indicates that the notes are slightly shortened but the bow does not leave the string.

TWO GERMAN DANCES

2

MOZART

VIOLIN

THE LARK

M. GLINKA
(1803-57)

Chester String Series

Graded Violin Pieces
Volume 2 (1st. Position)

Arranged and Edited by

Peggy Radmall

Extra Violin parts available

Chester Music
(A Music Sales Limited Company)
8/9 Frith Street, London, W1V 5TZ

Chester String Series

Graded Violin Pieces
Volume 1 (1st. Position)

Arranged and Edited by

Peggy Radmall

Extra Violin parts available

Chester Music
(A Music Sales Limited Company)
8/9 Frith Street, London, W1V 5TZ

TOWER HILL

GILES FARNABY
(*c.*1560-*c.*1600)

Allegretto

HIS REST

GILES FARNABY

GAVOTTE

G. F. HANDEL
(1685-1759)

CHANSON FAVORITE D'HENRI IV

Traditional

FINE
mf
dim.
p
pp
MUSETTE
p
cresc.
mf
p
cresc.
mf
dim.
p
cresc.
f

mf
cresc.
f
p
rit.
D.C. al Fine
dim.

MINUET AND TRIO

W. A. MOZART
(1756-91)

p
p
p
p
D.C. al Fine

THE St CATHERINE

JOHN BARRETT
(*c.* 1674–*c.* 1735)

Allegretto vivace

SARABAND

JOHN BARRETT
(*c.* 1674–*c.* 1735)

Andante espressivo

RIGAUDONS

HENRI DESMARETS
(*c.*1662-1741)

Allegro

p
cresc.
f
p
cresc.
f
p
cresc.
f
più f
cresc.
f
più f
tr
tr
p
p
rall.
cresc.
f
cresc.
f

TWO GERMAN DANCES

1

MOZART
(1756-91)

mf
mf
p
p
D. C. al fine
senza repetizione

TWO GERMAN DANCES

2

MOZART

D.C. al fine
senza repetizione

THE LARK

M. GLINKA
(1803-57)

Printed and bound in Great Britain by Caligraving Limited

7/05 (55703)

Chester String Series

Graded Violin Pieces
Volume 3 (1st–3rd Position)

Arranged and Edited by

Peggy Radmall

Extra Violin parts available

Chester Music